RAPHAEL GOMES'
EPIC KITCHEN ADVENTURES

PUBLISHED BY BLINK PUBLISHING
107-109 THE PLAZA,
535 KING'S ROAD,
CHELSEA HARBOUR,
LONDON, SW10 0SZ

WWW.BLINKPUBLISHING.CO.UK

FACEBOOK.COM/BLINKPUBLISHING
TWITTER.COM/BLINKPUBLISHING

9781910536193

A CIP CATALOGUE OF THIS BOOK IS AVAILABLE
FROM THE BRITISH LIBRARY.

DESIGN BY BLINK PUBLISHING

PRINTED AND BOUND BY UAB BALTO, LITHUANIA

1 3 5 7 9 10 8 6 4 2

PAPERS USED BY BLINK PUBLISHING ARE NATURAL, RECYCLABLE
PRODUCTS MADE FROM WOOD GROWN IN SUSTAINABLE FORESTS. THE MANU-
FACTURING PROCESSES CONFORM TO THE
ENVIRONMENTAL REGULATIONS OF THE COUNTRY OF ORIGIN.

BLINK PUBLISHING IS AN IMPRINT OF THE BONNIER PUBLISHING GROUP
WWW.BONNIERPUBLISHING.CO.UK

RAPHAEL GOMES'
EPIC
KITCHEN
ADVENTURES

TASTY TREATS READY IN MINUTES!

BLINK
bringing you closer

TO ANYONE WHO NEEDS A BREAK FROM THE REAL WORLD. I HOPE
THIS BOOK BRINGS YOU FUN. LAUGHTER AND GOOD MEMORIES.

THE EPIC KITCHEN ADVENTURES APP

SCAN HERE

EMBARK ON YOUR OWN CRAZY JOURNEY AND CREATE SOME OF YOUR OWN WONDERFUL TREATS WITH RAPHAEL GOMES' *EPIC KITCHEN ADVENTURES* BOOK AND APP, FEATURING AN EXCLUSIVE RECIPE AND NEVER-BEFORE-SEEN VIDEO CONTENT! THIS UNIQUE APP IS A FANTASTIC ADDITION TO RAPHAEL'S WONDERFUL YOUTUBE CHANNEL AND A BRILLIANT ACCESSORY TO HIS *EPIC KITCHEN ADVENTURES*.

ACCESS THE FREE APP FROM THE ITUNES APP STORE OR GOOGLE PLAY STORE, POINT YOUR DEVICE AT THE PAGES WITH THE 'SCAN HERE' ICONS AND RAPHAEL'S AMAZING FOOD HACKS AND VIDEOS WILL BE REVEALED ON THE DEVICE'S SCREEN.*

*THE APP REQUIRES AN INTERNET CONNECTION TO BE DOWNLOADED, AND CAN BE USED ON IPHONE, IPAD OR ANDROID DEVICES. FOR DIRECT LINKS TO DOWNLOAD THE APP AND FURTHER INFORMATION, VISIT WWW.BLINKPUBLISHING.CO.UK.

CONTENTS

INTRODUCTION

MY NAME IS RAPHAEL GOMES AND THIS IS MY FIRST BOOK, *EPIC KITCHEN ADVENTURES*.

I CURRENTLY LIVE IN LONDON BUT I WAS BORN IN A PORTUGUESE FAMILY WITH ONE YOUNGER SISTER. AND AS A TYPICALLY SOUTHERN EUROPEAN COUNTRY, FOOD WAS A BIG PART OF MY LIFE GROWING UP. MY PARENTS HAVE ALWAYS HOSTED BARBEQUES FOR BIG FAMILY GATHERINGS AND OUR TYPICAL CHRISTMAS ALWAYS INVOLVED AT LEAST 60 MEMBERS OF MY FAMILY HAVING DINNER AT MY GRANDMA'S HOUSE – LOTS OF PEOPLE SITTING AROUND A LARGE TABLE, WITH ENDLESS AMOUNTS OF WONDERFUL FOOD BEING SHARED. MY MUM HAS ALWAYS BEEN IN CHARGE OF DESSERTS AND SWEETS FOR THESE EVENTS AND I REMEMBER ALWAYS BEING BY HER SIDE WATCHING, HELPING AND ASKING FAR TOO MANY QUESTIONS.

ONE OF MY FIRST AND FAVOURITE CHILDHOOD MEMORIES WAS MAKING PANCAKES WITH MY MUM WHEN I WAS FIVE YEARS OLD. I CAN CLEARLY REMEMBER HOW FASCINATED AND EXCITED I WAS ABOUT THE WHOLE PROCESS – HOW YOU CAN MAKE SOMETHING SO AMAZING AND DELICIOUS OUT OF A FEW BASIC INGREDIENTS. I ALSO REMEMBER HOW MY MUM WOULD ALWAYS TAKE RECIPES TO THE NEXT LEVEL TO MAKE THEM MORE EXCITING AND MAGICAL. ALMOST EVERY TIME WE MADE PANCAKES, THEY ENDED UP AS RAINBOW PANCAKES. WE WOULD DIVIDE THE MIXTURE INTO DIFFERENT BOWLS AND ADD FOOD COLOURING – BLUE, RED, GREEN, YELLOW. THE FLAVOUR OF THE PANCAKES BY ITSELF WOULDN'T CHANGE BUT IT MADE THE WHOLE EXPERIENCE SO MUCH MORE ENJOYABLE AND MEMORABLE. I FELL IN LOVE WITH COOKING AND BAKING IN THAT UNCONVENTIONAL WAY. IT WAS FUN TO CREATE SOMETHING, BUT IT WAS EVEN MORE ENJOYABLE TO BREAK THE RULES AND PUSH RECIPES TO THE NEXT LEVEL TO MAKE SOMETHING EXTRA SPECIAL.

I GREW UP COOKING AND BAKING AS OFTEN AS I COULD. ALMOST EVERY SATURDAY NIGHT MY FRIENDS WOULD COME OVER TO MY HOUSE AND WE WOULD BAKE M&M COOKIES OR THE MOST AMAZING CHOCOLATE

MUG CAKES. THEN, AFTER DOCUMENTING ALL THE FUN WE HAD ON SOCIAL MEDIA, WE WOULD SIT DOWN AND ENJOY OUR CREATIONS WHILE WATCHING HORROR MOVIES IN SECRET.

WHEN I WAS 15 I FOUND THIS VIDEO-SHARING WEBSITE CALLED YOUTUBE. I ALWAYS ENJOYED GOING TO SCHOOL AND I HAD GOOD GRADES, BUT I ALWAYS FELT LIKE THERE WAS SOMETHING MISSING - LIKE A CONSTANT FEELING OF BOREDOM. SO I DECIDED TO START MAKING VIDEOS ON YOUTUBE AND SHARE SOME OF MY OPINIONS AND LIFE EXPERIENCES WITH OTHER USERS. NOT MANY PEOPLE WERE WATCHING BUT I FELT LIKE I FINALLY FOUND SOMETHING I WAS PASSIONATE ABOUT, SOMETHING TO LOOK FORWARD TO EVERY DAY WHEN I GOT HOME. WHETHER IT WAS FILMING A VIDEO OR READING THE COMMENTS ON MY RECENT POSTS, I HAD SOMETHING THAT MADE ME REALLY HAPPY.

ONE DAY I WAS TELLING MY MUM ABOUT MY VIDEOS AND THE IDEAS I WAS TRYING TO COME UP WITH, WHEN SHE ASKED ME WHY I HAD NEVER THOUGHT OF COMBINING MY VIDEOS WITH MY PASSION FOR COOKING? I DIDN'T HAVE AN ANSWER, BECAUSE EVEN I WAS SURPRISED THAT I NEVER THOUGHT OF THAT BEFORE. I EXPLAINED TO HER THAT WHILE I LOVE THOSE TWO THINGS, I DIDN'T WANT TO HAVE A SERIOUS AND OVERLY INSTRUCTIONAL COOKING SHOW. MY VIDEOS WERE SUPPOSED TO BE FUN AND COLOURFUL, AND NOT VERY TIME-CONSUMING; BUT BEFORE I COULD FINISH, MY MUM REACHED FOR HER RECIPE DRAWER AND GAVE ME A RECIPE FOR A TWO-MINUTE MICROWAVE CHOCOLATE CAKE IN A MUG WE HAD BEEN PERFECT-ING FOR THE LAST FEW WEEKS. THAT RECIPE BECAME MY FIRST EVER COOKING VIDEO, WHICH ENDED UP BECOMING `COOKING WITH RAPHAEL' - A SERIES OF VIDEOS THAT I'M STILL CREATING ON MY YOUTUBE CHANNEL TODAY. THE RESPONSE TO THE FIRST VIDEO WAS SO SURPRISING AND OVERWHELMINGLY POSITIVE, AND NEARLY 3 MILLION PEOPLE HAVE WATCHED IT SINCE I FIRST UPLOADED IT. I BEGAN TO GET MORE AND MORE REQUESTS FOR DIFFERENT COOKING VIDEOS AND I COULDN'T WAIT TO WORK ON MY NEXT CREA-TION. NUTELLA CUPCAKES, GIANT COOKIES, MICROWAVE PIZZA, ZEBRA CAKE AND CINNAMON-ROLL MUG CAKE ALL MADE AN APPEARANCE ON THE CHANNEL FOLLOWING MY FIRST EVER CHOCOLATE MUG CAKE ALL THOSE YEARS AGO.

I STARTED GETTING A LOT OF SUPPORTERS AND VIEWERS FROM ALL OVER THE WORLD, AND I WAS AMAZED HOW THE ONE THING UNITING US WAS OUR LOVE FOR FOOD IN A NOT-SO-CONVENTIONAL WAY. RAINBOW COOKIES, GIANT BISCUITS, PIZZA EVERYTHING - THE CRAZIER THE RECIPES AND VIDEOS, THE HAPPIER MY VIEWERS WOULD BE. I ABSOLUTELY LOVE THAT!

FOOD IS A VERY BIG PART OF MY LIFE. I BELIEVE YOU PUT A LITTLE BIT OF YOURSELF AND HOW YOU'RE FEELING INTO EVERY RECIPE AND HOPEFULLY THIS BOOK WILL SHOW THAT. IF YOU ARE FEELING ANGRY MAYBE IT'S TIME TO CRUSH SOME OREOS AND MAKE SOME DELICIOUS CHOCOLATE TRUFFLES. IF YOUR FRIENDS ARE AROUND AND YOU'RE ALL FEELING A LITTLE BIT BORED, MAYBE CREATING A NUTELLA MICROWAVE CAKE IS THE PERFECT WAY TO GET SOME ENTHUSIASM GOING.

THESE RECIPES ARE SIMPLE, FUN AND YOU CAN QUICKLY PUT THEM TOGETHER WITH A FEW INGREDIENTS YOU PROBABLY ALREADY OWN IN YOUR KITCHEN. YOU CAN BE CREATIVE AS YOU LIKE, BUT KEEP IN MIND SOME MUGS MIGHT BE LARGER THAN THE ONES I USED WHEN I PUT MY KITCHEN ADVENTURES TOGETHER. MY FAVOURITE MUG IS APPROXIMATELY 300ML AND I USE AN 800-WATT MICROWAVE, BUT DIFFERENT POWERS AND MUG SIZES MIGHT PRODUCE SLIGHTLY DIFFERENT RESULTS... SO KEEP AN EYE ON THINGS WHEN YOU'RE MAKING YOUR OWN ADVENTURE! THE RECIPES ARE PERFECT FOR A WEEKNIGHT WHEN YOU'RE HOME ALONE, CRAVING SOMETHING SWEET BUT DON'T WANT TO SPEND HOURS IN THE KITCHEN WASHING UP DISHES. THEY'RE ALSO GREAT FOR GROUP ACTIVITIES TO HELP YOU IMPROVE YOUR SLEEPOVERS AND GET A FEW LAUGHS WITH YOUR BEST FRIENDS.

THIS BOOK IS FOR MY VIEWERS WHO HAVE BEEN FOLLOWING ME FOR A WHILE, BUT, MOST IMPORTANTLY, THIS BOOK IS FOR MYSELF. I WISH I COULD HAVE OWNED THIS SELECTION OF RECIPES GROWING UP BECAUSE THE POSSIBILITIES AND FUN ARE ENDLESS. IT CELEBRATES EVERYTHING I LOVE ABOUT FOOD AND FRIENDSHIP, AND I AM SO EXCITED TO HAVE YOU READING THROUGH IT. GOOD LUCK EVERYBODY!

THE RECIPES

SCAN HERE

MUG CAKES

Flour

chocolate

CHOCOLATE MUG CAKE

INGREDIENTS

2 TABLESPOONS OF
WHITE SUGAR

2 TABLESPOONS OF
SELF-RAISING FLOUR

2 TABLESPOONS OF
COCOA POWDER

1 EGG

1 TABLESPOON OF OIL

1 TABLESPOON OF
MILK

CHOCOLATE CHIPS

INSTRUCTIONS

1. COMBINE ALL THE INGREDIENTS, ADDING
   THEM IN THE ORDER LISTED EXCEPT FOR
   THE CHOCOLATE CHIPS.

2. MIX THEM TOGETHER IN THE MUG USING
   A FORK.

3. SPRINKLE SOME FLOUR ON THE CHOCOLATE
   CHIPS TO MAKE SURE THEY DON'T SINK TO
   THE BOTTOM.

4. ADD THEM TO THE MUG MIXTURE.

5. MICROWAVE FOR ABOUT 2 MINUTES OR
   UNTIL IT STOPS RISING.

6. ENJOY YOUR QUICK TREAT WITH A SMILE
   ON YOUR FACE!

RAPHA'S TIP

INSTEAD OF USING CHOCOLATE CHIPS,
CHOP YOUR FAVOURITE CHOCOLATE
BAR INTO SMALL PIECES.

BANANA MUG CAKE

- 1 TABLESPOON OF MILK

- 1 EGG

- 1 TABLESPOON OF MELTED BUTTER

- 1 MASHED MEDIUM-SIZED BANANA

- ¼ TEASPOON OF VANILLA ESSENCE

- 3 TABLESPOONS OF PLAIN FLOUR

- 3 TABLESPOONS OF BROWN SUGAR

- ½ TEASPOON OF BAKING POWDER

INSTRUCTIONS

1. COMBINE ALL THE INGREDIENTS, ADDING THEM IN THE ORDER LISTED, EXCEPT FOR THE CHOCOLATE CHIPS.

2. MIX THE INGREDIENTS TOGETHER IN THE MUG USING A FORK.

3. SPRINKLE SOME FLOUR ON THE CHOCOLATE CHIPS TO MAKE SURE THEY DON'T SINK TO THE BOTTOM.

4. ADD THEM TO THE MUG MIXTURE.

5. MICROWAVE FOR ABOUT 2 MINUTES OR UNTIL IT STOPS RISING.

6. NOW SMILE BIG BECAUSE YOU JUST MADE A DELICIOUS CAKE. TIME TO TAKE SOME PICTURES!

RAPHA'S TIP

SERVE YOUR CAKE WITH A SCOOP OF PEANUT BUTTER CUP ICE CREAM FOR ULTIMATE DELICIOUSNESS.

COVER THE TOP OF YOUR BANANAS WITH PLASTIC WRAP AND THEY WILL LAST FOUR OR FIVE DAYS LONGER

LINE A MUFFIN TRAY
WITH BACON
AND POUR SOME
WHISKED EGGS
INTO IT. 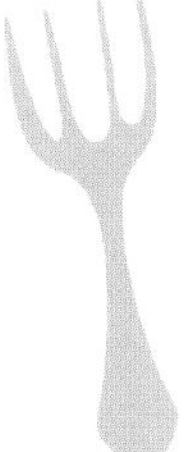
BAKE IN THE OVEN
FOR 20 MINUTES
AND YOU'VE GOT A
PERFECT BREAKFAST
ON THE GO

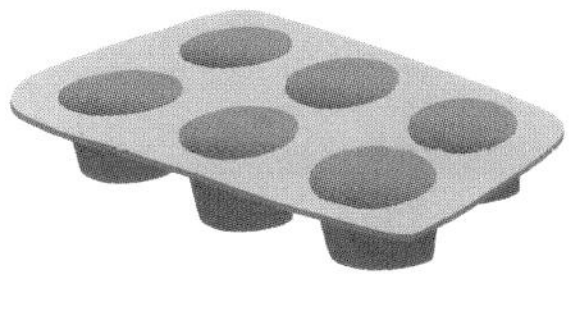

NUTELLA MUG CAKE

INGREDIENTS

4 TABLESPOONS OF
SELF-RAISING FLOUR

2 TABLESPOONS OF
SUGAR

1 EGG

2 TABLESPOONS OF
COCOA POWDER

1 TABLESPOON OF HOT-
CHOCOLATE MIX

3 TABLESPOONS OF
NUTELLA

3 TABLESPOONS OF
MILK

3 TABLESPOONS OF
VEGETABLE OIL

INSTRUCTIONS

1. COMBINE ALL INGREDIENTS IN A MUG USING A FORK.

2. WHEN SMOOTH, MICROWAVE FOR 1 TO 2 MINUTES.

3. CHECK IF IT'S COOKED; IF NOT MICRO-WAVE FOR A FEW MORE SECONDS UNTIL PERFECTION.

RAPHA'S TIP

TOP YOUR MUG CAKE WITH SOME
WHIPPED CREAM AND SPRINKLE SOME HOT
CHOCOLATE MIX OVER THE TOP.

MUG CHOCOLATE CHIP COOKIE

INGREDIENTS

1 TABLESPOON OF
MELTED BUTTER

1 TABLESPOON OF
SUGAR

1 TABLESPOON OF
BROWN SUGAR

3 TABLESPOONS OF
PLAIN FLOUR

1 EGG YOLK

¼ TEASPOON OF
VANILLA EXTRACT

CHOCOLATE CHIPS

INSTRUCTIONS

1. FIND A WIDE MUG OR BOWL, RATHER THAN A TALL ONE AS WE'RE MAKING A COOKIE AND NOT A CAKE.

2. PLACE THE MELTED BUTTER, SUGARS AND VANILLA EXTRACT IN THE MUG AND STIR.

3. ADD THE EGG YOLK, MAKING SURE THE BUTTER MIXTURE ISN'T TOO HOT.

4. ADD THE FLOUR AND STIR UNTIL YOU GET A COOKIE DOUGH CONSISTENCY.

5. ADD THE CHOCOLATE CHIPS.

6. MICROWAVE IT FOR 30 SECONDS TO 1 MINUTE.

7. IF YOU LIKE A DELICIOUS, SOFT, GOOEY COOKIE, MAKE SURE NOT TO OVERCOOK IT BY CHECKING EVERY 20 SECONDS.

RAPHA'S TIP

USE A MIXTURE OF DARK, MILK AND WHITE CHOCOLATE CHIPS FOR EXTRA AWESOMENESS!

REESE'S PEANUT BUTTER MUG

INGREDIENTS

¼ CUP OF PLAIN FLOUR

2 TABLESPOONS OF COCOA POWDER

2 TABLESPOONS OF SUGAR

¼ OF A TEASPOON OF BAKING POWDER

¼ CUP OF MILK

1 TABLESPOON OF MELTED BUTTER

1 MEDIUM SCOOP OF SMOOTH PEANUT BUTTER

2 REESE'S PEANUT BUTTER CUPS

INSTRUCTIONS

1. GRAB YOUR FAVOURITE MUG AND ADD THE FLOUR, COCOA POWDER, SUGAR AND BAKING POWDER.

2. GIVE IT A QUICK MIX.

3. ADD THE MILK AND MELTED BUTTER AND COMBINE REALLY WELL.

4. SCOOP ONE MEDIUM SPOON OF SMOOTH PEANUT BUTTER AND ADD A CRUSHED REESE'S BUTTER CUP TO THE SPOON.

5. DROP IT RIGHT IN THE MIDDLE OF YOUR MUG CAKE MIXTURE AND SMOOTH OUT THE TOP SO YOU CAN'T SEE THE PEANUT BUTTER FILLING.

6. COOK IT FOR ABOUT 2 MINUTES IN THE MICROWAVE AND IT'S READY TO EAT!

RAPHA'S TIP

I ALWAYS TOP MY CAKE WITH ONE MORE CRUSHED REESE'S PEANUT BUTTER CUP BECAUSE I'M PRETTY SURE THAT'S WHAT DREAMS ARE MADE OF.

SCAN HERE

WHITE CHOCOLATE AND OREO MUG CAKE

INGREDIENTS

¼ CUP OF WHITE CHOCOLATE

4 TABLESPOONS OF MILK

¼ CUP OF FLOUR

¼ TEASPOON OF BAKING POWDER

2 OREO COOKIES

INSTRUCTIONS

1. MICROWAVE THE WHITE CHOCOLATE AND 3 TABLESPOONS OF MILK FOR 30 SECONDS IN A MUG.

2. STIR THE MIXTURE UNTIL SMOOTH.

3. ADD IN BAKING POWDER AND FLOUR, AND COMBINE WELL.

4. ADD THE FINAL TABLESPOON OF MILK AND STIR.

5. PLACE THE 2 OREO COOKIES IN THE MIXTURE AND BREAK THEM INTO SMALL PIECES.

6. MICROWAVE FOR ABOUT 1 MINUTE.

RAPHA'S TIP

TOP YOUR MUG CAKE WITH SOMETHING TASTY LIKE SOME CRUSHED OREOS OR CHOCOLATE SPRINKLES!

CHOCOLATE BROWNIE IN A MUG

INGREDIENTS

2 TABLESPOONS OF WATER

2 TABLESPOONS OF SOFT BUTTER

4 TABLESPOONS OF SUGAR

3 TABLESPOONS OF COCOA POWDER

4 TABLESPOONS OF PLAIN FLOUR

½ TEASPOON OF VANILLA EXTRACT

SALT

WALNUTS (OPTIONAL)

INSTRUCTIONS

1. THIS RECIPE IS PERFECT FOR A LARGE ESPRESSO-TYPE MUG, BUT A REGULAR MUG WORKS JUST AS WELL.

2. ADD WATER, BUTTER AND VANILLA EXTRACT TO YOUR MUG, STIRRING REALLY WELL.

3. NOW ADD THE SUGAR, COCOA POWDER, FLOUR, SALT AND WALNUTS AND MIX UNTIL EVERYTHING'S WELL COMBINED.

4. MICROWAVE FOR 1 TO 2 MINUTES, CHECKING REGULARLY TO NOT OVER-COOK.

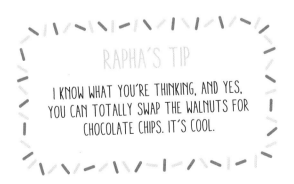

RAPHA'S TIP

I KNOW WHAT YOU'RE THINKING, AND YES, YOU CAN TOTALLY SWAP THE WALNUTS FOR CHOCOLATE CHIPS. IT'S COOL.

PEANUT BUTTER MUG CAKE

INGREDIENTS

4 TABLESPOONS OF
PLAIN FLOUR

¼ TEASPOON OF
BAKING POWDER

4 TABLESPOONS OF
SUGAR

4 TABLESPOONS OF
ALMOND MILK

3 TABLESPOONS OF
PEANUT BUTTER

¼ TEASPOON OF
VANILLA EXTRACT

NUTELLA

INSTRUCTIONS

1. FIND YOUR FAVOURITE MUG.

2. WITH A FORK COMBINE ALL INGREDIENTS,
   APART FROM THE NUTELLA, IN THE MUG.

3. MICROWAVE FOR ABOUT 1 MINUTE AND
   CHECK IF IT NEEDS A FEW MORE SECONDS.

4. DRIZZLE SOME NUTELLA ON TOP FOR THE
   MOST AMAZING COMBINATION!

DELICIOUS SPONGE MUG CAKE

INGREDIENTS

2 TABLESPOONS OF
MELTED BUTTER

2 TABLESPOONS OF
SUGAR

5 TABLESPOONS OF
FLOUR

½ TEASPOON OF
BAKING POWDER

2 TABLESPOONS OF
MILK

1 EGG

INSTRUCTIONS

1. COMBINE ALL INGREDIENTS IN YOUR
   FAVOURITE MUG USING A FORK.

2. MICROWAVE IT FOR 40 TO 60 SECONDS
   CHECKING CAREFULLY.

3. ENJOY YOUR QUICK AND DELICIOUS
   SPONGE CAKE.

RAPHA'S TIP

THIS IS THE PERFECT CAKE TO TOP WITH
FRESH STRAWBERRIES AND CREAM!

CINNAMON ROLL MUG CAKE

INGREDIENTS

- 2 TABLESPOONS OF APPLE SAUCE
- 1 TABLESPOON OF VEGETABLE OIL
- ½ TABLESPOON OF MILK
- ¼ TEASPOON OF VANILLA EXTRACT
- ¼ CUP, PLUS A TABLESPOON, OF PLAIN FLOUR
- 2 AND ½ TABLESPOONS OF LIGHT BROWN SUGAR
- ¾ TEASPOON OF GROUND CINNAMON
- 1 DASH OF GROUND NUTMEG
- ¼ TEASPOON OF BAKING POWDER

INSTRUCTIONS

1. FIND A WIDE MUG RATHER THAN A TALL ONE, AS THIS RECIPE DOESN'T RISE.

2. COMBINE ALL THE WET INGREDIENTS FIRST AND STIR WITH A FORK.

3. ADD THE DRY INGREDIENTS AND COMBINE ONCE AGAIN.

4. MICROWAVE IT FOR ABOUT 1 MINUTE CHECKING REGULARLY.

SCAN HERE

RAPHA'S TIP

TOP THE CAKE WITH SOME DELICIOUS ICING FOR THE CLASSIC CINNAMON ROLL FLAVOUR.

COFFEE AND CHOCOLATE MUG

INGREDIENTS

3 TABLESPOONS OF
PLAIN FLOUR

2 TABLESPOONS OF HOT
CHOCOLATE MIX

1 TABLESPOON OF
INSTANT COFFEE
POWDER

3 TABLESPOONS OF
SUGAR

¼ TEASPOON OF
BAKING POWDER

2 TABLESPOONS OF MILK

1 EGG

2 TABLESPOONS OF OIL

INSTRUCTIONS

1. MIX THE DRY INGREDIENTS IN YOUR MUG.

2. ADD THE EGG, MILK AND OIL, AND STIR
   WITH A FORK UNTIL SMOOTH.

3. MICROWAVE IT FOR 60 TO 90 SECONDS,
   CHECKING REGULARLY AFTER 1 MINUTE.

4. DUST SOME ICING SUGAR ON TOP.

RAPHA'S TIP
THIS LOOKS EVEN MORE AMAZING IF
YOU SERVE IT IN A TRANSPARENT
ESPRESSO MUGS.

POUR DROPS OF
FOOD COLOURING
ONTO THE SURFACE OF A
SLIGHTLY CRACKED HARD-BOILED EGG
FOR A BEAUTIFUL EFFECT

SLICE A ROUND TUB OF
ICE CREAM
AND PLACE IT
IN BETWEEN
TWO COOKIES
FOR AN IMMEDIATE
ICE CREAM
SANDWICH

SCAN HERE

PIZZA
EVERYTHING

QUICKEST PIZZA DOUGH EVER!

MAKES 1 MEDIUM PIZZA

INGREDIENTS

150G OF PLAIN FLOUR

3G OF ACTIVE DRY YEAST

10ML OF VEGETABLE OIL

2G OF SALT

5G OF WHITE SUGAR

95ML OF WARM WATER (45°C)

INSTRUCTIONS

1. ADD THE DRY YEAST AND WHITE SUGAR TO YOUR WARM WATER (MAKE SURE IT'S NOT TOO HOT).

2. LET IT SIT FOR 1 OR 2 MINUTES.

3. NOW COMBINE THE MIXTURE WITH THE REST OF THE INGREDIENTS IN A LARGE BOWL.

4. WHEN IT STARTS TO GET REALLY THICK IT'S TIME TO USE YOUR HANDS!

5. SPRINKLE A SURFACE WITH FLOUR AND WORK THE DOUGH WITH YOUR HANDS UNTIL IT'S SMOOTH AND ALL THE INGREDIENTS ARE INCORPORATED.

6. YOU CAN USE IT STRAIGHT AWAY OR LET IT SIT IN A WARM PLACE TO RISE FOR 20 MINUTES!

RAPHA'S TIP

THIS RECIPE REALLY IS AMAZING BECAUSE IT DOESN'T INVOLVE HOURS AND HOURS OF WAITING AROUND. I FIND THAT IT WORKS THE BEST WHEN YOU MAKE THIN AND CRISPY PIZZAS BUT YOU CAN DEFINITELY ALSO USE IT FOR A THICK PIZZA BASE!

SCAN HERE

ONE-MINUTE MICROWAVE MINI-PIZZAS

MAKES 10 MINI-PIZZAS

INGREDIENTS

10 SALTINE CRACKERS
(TUC STYLE)

TOMATO PASTE
OR TOMATO SAUCE

OREGANO

GARLIC POWDER

OLIVE OIL

SALT

HOT SAUCE OR PEPPER
FLAKES

MOZZARELLA CHEESE

INSTRUCTIONS

1. IN A BOWL, COMBINE THE TOMATO, OREGANO, GARLIC POWDER, SALT AND HOT SAUCE. DRIZZLE SOME OLIVE OIL TO FINISH.

2. ADJUST MEASUREMENTS ACCORDING TO TASTE AND HOW MUCH SAUCE YOU WANT ON YOUR MINI-PIZZAS.

3. INDIVIDUALLY SPOON THE MIXTURE ONTO THE SALTINE CRACKERS.

4. TOP IT WITH MOZZARELLA CHEESE AND/ OR YOUR FAVOURITE PIZZA TOPPINGS.

5. MICROWAVE IT FOR ABOUT 1 MINUTE, BUT DO NOT OVERCOOK THE CRACKERS.

6. ENJOY THE DELICIOUS FLAVOUR OF A CLASSIC AND SPEEDY PIZZA!

RAPHA'S TIP

THIS IS THE PERFECT AFTER-CLASS SNACK WHEN YOU'RE TOO HUNGRY FOR SOMETHING SAVOURY, BUT IT'S NOT QUITE DINNERTIME YET.

CUT MULTIPLE STRIKES ON A POTATO AND BAKE IT FOR 20 MINUTES WITH SOME BUTTER.

ADD CREAM, CHEDDAR CHEESE AND BAKE IT FOR ANOTHER 20 MINUTES.

YOU'VE GOT THE MOST DELICIOUS AND CRISPY BAKED POTATO

TURN A CUPCAKE TRAY UPSIDE DOWN, GREASE IT AND COVER THE TOPS WITH SOME COOKIE DOUGH. YOU'LL END UP WITH PERFECT COOKIE BASKETS TO SERVE WITH CUSTARD OR CREAM AND YOUR FAVOURITE FRUITS. THEY ARE THE EASIEST MINI TARTS!

PEPPERONI CHEESE ROLL-UPS

MAKES 6 ROLL-UPS

INGREDIENTS

FRESH PIZZA
DOUGH (SEE P. 49)

8 CHEESE STICKS

1 PACKET OF SLICED
PEPPERONI

4 TABLESPOONS OF
MELTED BUTTER

½ TEASPOON OF
OREGANO

¼ TEASPOON OF
GARLIC POWDER

INSTRUCTIONS

1. MY QUICKEST PIZZA DOUGH IS IDEAL FOR THIS RECIPE. PREHEAT OVEN TO 180°C.

2. ROLL OUT THE PIZZA DOUGH IN A CIRCLE AND SLICE IT INTO TRIANGLES.

3. PLACE PEPPERONI AND CHEESE STICKS ON THE WIDER SIDE OF THE TRIANGLE.

4. ROLL INTO A CROISSANT SHAPE.

5. BAKE ROLL-UPS FOR 10 TO 15 MINUTES OR UNTIL CRISPY AND BROWN.

6. IN A SMALL BOWL, COMBINE THE MELTED BUTTER, OREGANO AND GARLIC POWDER TO MAKE A DELICIOUS GLAZE.

7. AS THE ROLL-UPS COME OUT OF THE OVEN, BRUSH THEM WITH THE MIXTURE AND THEY WILL IMMEDIATELY ABSORB MOST OF THE FLAVOUR.

8. ENJOY THE MOST AMAZING PIZZA ROLL-UPS!

RAPHA'S TIP

THIS IS ACTUALLY THE GREATEST ALTERNATIVE TO GARLIC BREAD AND ROLLING THESE UP IS TOO MUCH FUN.

SCAN HERE

PIZZA CUPCAKES

INGREDIENTS

FRESH PIZZA
DOUGH (SEE P. 49)

1 GREEN PEPPER

½ ONION

150G MUSHROOM

75G BLACK OLIVES

150G TOMATO
PUREE OR PASTE

½ TEASPOON OF
OREGANO

¼ TEASPOON OF
GARLIC POWDER

SALT

100G GRATED
MOZZARELLA
CHEESE

INSTRUCTIONS

1. MY QUICKEST PIZZA DOUGH IS IDEAL FOR THIS RECIPE. PREHEAT OVEN TO 180°C.

2. GREASE A CUPCAKE TRAY WITH BUTTER OR NON-STICK SPRAY AND SPRINKLE SOME FLOUR.

3. ROLL OUT THE PIZZA DOUGH AND, USING A GLASS, TRY TO MAKE CIRCLES SLIGHTLY BIGGER THAN THE CUPCAKE MOLDS.

4. CHOP THE ONION, MUSHROOM, PEPPER AND OLIVES.

5. COMBINE THE TOMATO PUREE WITH THE GARLIC, OREGANO AND SOME SALT.

6. PLACE THE DOUGH CIRCLES ON THE CUPCAKE MOULDS.

7. TOP IT WITH THE TOMATO SAUCE AND THE CHOPPED VEGETABLES.

8. SPRINKLE WITH MOZZARELLA CHEESE.

9. BAKE IT FOR ABOUT 25 MINUTES OR UNTIL THE DOUGH IS GOLDEN AND BROWN.

RAPHA'S TIP

YOU CAN USE ANY TOPPINGS YOU WANT FOR THIS RECIPE. IT'S ALSO A GREAT ON-THE-GO SNACK IF YOU'RE RUNNING LATE FOR CLASS OR WORK.

≡PIZZA CAKE≡

PIZZA BASE (VANILLA SPONGE)

SERVES 8

INGREDIENTS

115G OF BUTTER

150G OF WHITE SUGAR

4 EGG YOLKS

90ML MILK

4ML OF VANILLA EXTRACT

135G OF SELF-RAISING FLOUR

2G OF SALT

INSTRUCTIONS

1. PREHEAT OVEN TO 175°C.

2. GREASE AND FLOUR AROUND THE PAN.

3. IN A LARGE BOWL, CREAM TOGETHER THE BUTTER AND SUGAR UNTIL LIGHT AND FLUFFY.

4. BEAT IN THE EGG YOLKS, THEN STIR IN THE VANILLA.

5. BEAT IN THE MILK.

6. SIFT THE FLOUR AND ADD SALT.

7. COMBINE EVERYTHING WITHOUT OVER-MIXING IT.

8. BAKE FOR 30 TO 35 MINUTES AND COOL FOR 15 MINUTES, BEFORE APPLYING THE TOPPING.

RAPHA'S TIP

AFTER YOU HAVE YOUR VANILLA SPONGE PIZZA BASE, IT'S TIME TO MAKE THE CREAMIEST AND SWEETEST PIZZA SAUCE (CHECK OUT THE NEXT PAGE)I SPREAD IT ON THE CAKE ONCE IT'S COOL!

PIZZA SAUCE

INGREDIENTS

60G OF SOFT BUTTER

1ML OF VANILLA EXTRACT

120G OF CONFECTIONER'S SUGAR

MILK (OPTIONAL)

RED FOOD COLOURING

INSTRUCTIONS

1. CREAM ALL THE INGREDIENTS TOGETHER REALLY WELL.

2. ADD MILK, BUT ONLY IF YOU FIND THE FROSTING TOO THICK AND DIFFICULT TO SPREAD.

RAPHA'S TIP

FINALLY ALL YOU NEED ARE YOUR PIZZA TOPPINGS! DON'T WORRY THIS IS THE EASIEST AND MOST FUN PART! CHECK OUT THE NEXT PAGE... SPRINKLE THESE FAKE PIZZA TOPPINGS ON THE PIZZA SAUCE AND VOILÁ :) PIZZA CAKE IS COMPLETE!

PIZZA TOPPINGS

INGREDIENTS

WHITE FONDANT

FOOD COLOURING

WHITE CHOCOLATE

INSTRUCTIONS

1. INCORPORATE THE FOOD COLOURING INTO THE FONDANT TO MAKE VIBRANT COLOURS.

2. ATTEMPT TO MAKE FAKE PEPPERONI AND CHEESE.

3. USE THE WHITE CHOCOLATE AND A CHEESE GRATER TO CREATE THE ILLUSION OF PARMESAN CHEESE.

4. BE CREATIVE AND HAVE LOTS OF FUN.

CANDY PIZZA WITH COOKIE DOUGH BASE

SERVES 6

INGREDIENTS

250G PLAIN FLOUR

½ TEASPOON OF BIRCARBONATE OF SODA

½ TEASPOON OF SALT

170G OF MELTED UNSALTED BUTTER

200G OF SOFT BROWN SUGAR

1 TEASPOON OF VANILLA EXTRACT

1 EGG

1 EGG YOLK

150G MILK CHOCOLATE CHIPS

INSTRUCTIONS

1. PREHEAT OVEN TO 180°C.

2. MIX TOGETHER THE DRY INGREDIENTS AND SET ASIDE.

3. CREAM THE BUTTER AND SUGAR IN A SEPARATE BOWL AND ONCE INCORPORATED ADD THE EGG AND EGG YOLK.

4. ADD THE DRY INGREDIENTS TO THE PREVIOUS MIXTURE FOLLOWED BY THE CHOCOLATE CHIPS.

5. STIR UNTIL IT COMES TOGETHER AND SPREAD OUT THE MIXTURE ONTO A BAKING TRAY LINED WITH PARCHMENT PAPER.

6. COOK FOR 25 MINUTES.

7. ADD YOUR DESIRED CANDY TOPPINGS AND FINISH COOKING FOR ANOTHER 5 TO 10 MINUTES. DON'T FORGET TO USE NUTELLA AS PIZZA SAUCE.

RAPHA'S TIP

MALTESERS, WHITE CHOCOLATE BUTTONS, AND KINDER EGG CHOCOLATE ARE ALL GREAT TOPPINGS FOR THIS, BUT MY ULTIMATE FAVOURITE IS A FEW SLICES OF MARSHMALLOW.

NUTELLA PIZZA

SERVES 4

INGREDIENTS

1 EGG YOLK

2 TABLESPOONS OF WHITE SUGAR

WHITE CHOCOLATE BUTTONS

MILK CHOCOLATE CHIPS

NUTELLA

PIZZA DOUGH OR PIZZA BASE

INSTRUCTIONS

1. PREHEAT OVEN TO 180°C.

2. ROLL OUT YOUR PIZZA DOUGH INTO A REGULAR-SIZED PIZZA.

3. WHISK THE EGG YOLK AND SUGAR AND BRUSH IT ON THE PIZZA BASE.

4. BAKE IT FOR 15 TO 20 MINUTES OR UNTIL GOLDEN BROWN.

5. AS SOON AS THE PIZZA IS OUT OF THE OVEN, SPREAD NUTELLA ON IT. IT SHOULD BE EASY AS IT'S STILL WARM.

6. APPLY THE CHOCOLATE BUTTONS AND CHOCOLATE CHIPS AND LET IT SOFTEN A LITTLE BIT.

7. FINISH OFF WITH THE RASPBERRIES FOR SOME FRESHNESS.

8. ENJOY THE SWEETEST NUTELLA PIZZA, SURPRISINGLY MADE WITH ACTUAL PIZZA DOUGH.

SCAN HERE

PIZZA TARTS

MAKES 12 PIZZA TARTS

INGREDIENTS

1 PACKET OF PUFF PASTRY

PIZZA SAUCE

1 CUP OF SHREDDED MOZZARELLA

SLICED ONION AND PEPPERS

ITALIAN SEASONING

INSTRUCTIONS

1. LINE UP SOME BAKING SHEETS OR PARCHMENT PAPER AND PLACE THIN SQUARES OF PASTRY ON IT (2 X 2 INCHES IS IDEAL, BUT YOU CAN MAKE GIANT ONES AS WELL).

2. SPOON 1 GENEROUS TEASPOON OF PIZZA SAUCE.

3. SPRINKLE WITH ONION, PEPPERS AND SHREDDED MOZZARELLA. TOP IT WITH SOME SEASONING.

4. BAKE IN THE OVEN FOR 15 MINUTES OR UNTIL PASTRY IS PUFFED AND GOLDEN.

5. TEXT SOME FRIENDS AND INVITE THEM OVER TO TRY THESE TASTY TREATS. OR STAY AT HOME AND EAT THE WHOLE THING YOURSELF… WE'VE ALL BEEN THERE ;)

RAPHA'S TIP

THESE TASTE SO DELICIOUS AND ARE SO EASY TO MAKE, PUFF PASTRY COOKS SO QUICKLY MAKING IT A GREAT ALTERNATIVE TO PIZZA DOUGH. HAVE FUN!

TURN A CUPCAKE TRAY
UPSIDE DOWN
AND COVER IT WITH
ALUMINIUM FOIL.
WRAP BACON AROUND
THE INVERTED CUPS
AND BAKE IT
FOR 15 MINUTES.
YOU'VE JUST CREATED A
BACON BASKET!

HANG YOUR **TORTILLA** ON THE SIDES OF THE RACKS WHILE THEY BAKE **IN THE OVEN** FOR THE PERFECT **TACO SHELL.**

SCAN HERE

COOKIES & BISCUITS

UNICORN POO COOKIES

MAKES 8 COOKIES

INGREDIENTS

170G OF SOFT BUTTER

200G OF WHITE SUGAR

2 EGGS

310G OF PLAIN FLOUR

5G OF BAKING POWDER

3G SALT

3ML OF VANILLA EXTRACT

STAR SPRINKLES

EDIBLE GLITTER

FOOD COLOURING

INSTRUCTIONS

1. PREHEAT OVEN TO 200°C.

2. CREAM THE BUTTER AND SUGAR UNTIL SMOOTH AND LIGHT.

3. BEAT IN THE EGGS AND VANILLA EXTRACT. STIR IN THE FLOUR, BAKING POWDER AND SALT, AND LET IT REST FOR A FEW MINUTES.

4. DIVIDE DOUGH INTO 4 EQUAL SECTIONS AND INCORPORATE FOOD COLOURING INTO EACH, WORKING THE DOUGH WITH YOUR HANDS.

5. STRETCH EACH PIECE OF DOUGH INTO THIN LOGS AND THEN PRESS THEM INTO ONE BIGGER LOG, COMBINING THE FOUR COLOURS.

6. CUT ACCORDING TO THE AMOUNT OF COOKIES YOU WISH TO MAKE AND TWIST EACH ONE, MAKING A RAINBOW SPIRAL EFFECT.

7. SHAPE THEM INTO POOP-LIKE FORMS AND BAKE THEM FOR 10 MINUTES.

8. DECORATE THEM WITH STAR-SHAPED SPRINKLES AND EDIBLE GLITTER FOR AN EXTRA MAGICAL TOUCH.

GIANT NUTELLA BISCUIT

SERVES 6

INGREDIENTS

340G OF PEANUT BUTTER

260G OF WHITE SUGAR

1 EGG

1 JAR OF NUTELLA

INSTRUCTIONS

1. PREHEAT OVEN TO 180°C.

2. LEAVE THE NUTELLA TO ONE SIDE AND COMBINE ALL THE INGREDIENTS IN A LARGE BOWL.

3. SHAPE YOUR GIANT BISCUIT INTO A FLAT VOLCANO AND MAKE SURE THERE'S A HOLE IN THE MIDDLE TO SPREAD THE NUTELLA.

4. BAKE IT FOR 20 TO 30 MINUTES OR UNTIL GOLDEN AND BROWN.

5. ONCE IT COOLS DOWN AND IT GETS A BIT TOUGHER, SPREAD AS MUCH NUTELLA AS YOU DESIRE IN THE CENTRE OF YOUR VOLCANO COOKIE.

6. TAKE A FEW PICTURES OF YOURSELF DIGGING INTO YOUR AWESOME GIANT NUTELLA BISCUIT!

RAPHA'S TIP

YOU CAN ALSO USE THIS RECIPE TO MAKE SMALL REGULAR SIZED ONES, THEY ARE SO EASY AND YET THE BEST BISCUITS YOU'LL EVER TRY! #BISCUITGOALS

CRUSH SOME OREOS
AND PLACE THEM INTO
AN ICE CUBE MOULD.
FILL UP THE ICE MOULDS
WITH MILK AND PLACE
IN THE FREEZER.
ADD IT TO YOUR COFFEE
FOR A QUICK TASTE OF
DELICIOUSNESS.

QUICKLY SAUTÉ SOME PEPPERONI, GARLIC, PARSLEY AND PEPPER FLAKES IN SOME BUTTER AND OLIVE OIL.

ROLL OUT THE PIZZA DOUGH, CUT IT INTO STRIPS AND TIE THOSE STRIPS INTO KNOTS.

BAKE FOR 25 MINUTES AT 220°C. TOSS THE KNOTS IN PEPPERONI GARLIC BUTTER FOR THE MOST AMAZING SNACK.

GIANT CHOCOLATE CHIP COOKIE

SERVES 6

INGREDIENTS

150G OF SOFT BUTTER

140G OF WHITE SUGAR

140G OF BROWN SUGAR

1 EGG

1 EGG YOLK

7ML OF VANILLA EXTRACT

250G OF PLAIN FLOUR

3G OF BAKING SODA

7ML OF HOT WATER

2G OF SALT

200G OF CHOCOLATE CHIPS

80G OF CRUSHED FROSTED FLAKES

INSTRUCTIONS

1. PREHEAT OVEN TO 175°C.

2. CREAM THE BUTTER, WHITE SUGAR AND BROWN SUGAR UNTIL SMOOTH.

3. BEAT IN THE EGGS AND VANILLA.

4. DISSOLVE THE BAKING SODA IN HOT WATER AND ADD IT TO THE MIXTURE.

5. ADD THE FLOUR, SALT, CHOCOLATE CHIPS AND FROSTED FLAKES AND STIR WITHOUT MIXING TOO MUCH.

6. NOW IT'S THE FUN PART: MAKE YOUR GIANT COOKIE AND PLACE IT ON TO PARCHMENT PAPER.

7. BAKE IT FOR 15 TO 25 MINUTES OR UNTIL THE EDGES ARE GOLDEN BROWN.

EMOJI SUGAR COOKIES

MAKES 12 COOKIES

INGREDIENTS

170G PLAIN FLOUR

2G BAKING SODA

1G OF BAKING POWDER

115G OF SOFTENED BUTTER

150G OF WHITE SUGAR

½ AN EGG

4ML OF VANILLA EXTRACT

COLOURED FONDANT

BLACK ICING TUBE FOR DETAILS

INSTRUCTIONS

1. PREHEAT OVEN TO 185°C.

2. IN A LARGE BOWL, COMBINE THE DRY INGREDIENTS (FLOUR, BAKING SODA AND BAKING POWDER) AND SET TO ONE SIDE.

3. CREAM THE SUGAR AND BUTTER UNTIL NICE AND SMOOTH. BEAT IN THE EGG AND VANILLA. BEAT IN THE DRY MIXTURE FROM BEFORE.

4. PLACE THE MIXTURE ON SOME PARCHMENT PAPER AND ATTEMPT TO FORM TINY BALLS WITH THE DOUGH.

5. BAKE THEM FROM 8 TO 12 MINUTES OR UNTIL GOLDEN. LET THEM COOL DOWN A LITTLE BIT.

6. USE COLOURED FONDANT AND FROST-ING TO DECORATE THE EMOJIS. A TUBE OF BLACK ICING IS GREAT FOR DETAILS AND A MORE POLISHED LOOK.

7. BE CREATIVE AND HAVE FUN!

CHAI TEA COOKIES*

MAKES 16 COOKIES

INGREDIENTS

250G OF WHITE SUGAR

150G BUTTER

2 EGG YOLKS

2ML VANILLA EXTRACT

210G OF PLAIN FLOUR

3G OF BAKING SODA

1 BAG OF CHAI TEA (OR YOUR FAVOURITE TEA)

INSTRUCTIONS

1. PREHEAT OVEN TO 180°C AND ALIGN TWO SHEETS OF PARCHMENT PAPER.

2. CREAM THE SUGAR AND BUTTER. ADD THE EGG YOLKS AND VANILLA, BEATING IN.

3. ADD THE DRY INGREDIENTS (FLOUR, BAKING SODA AND CHAI TEA) AND STIR.

4. SMELL THE DOUGH AT THIS POINT BECAUSE IT'S ALMOST MAGICAL!

5. PLACE DOUGH BALLS APART FROM EACH OTHER ON THE COOKIE SHEETS AND BAKE FOR 10 TO 12 MINUTES OR UNTIL THE CRUST HAS CRACKED.

*RAPHA'S FAVOURITE COOKIES

SCAN HERE

NO-BAKE OREO TRUFFLES

MAKES 36 TRUFFLES

INGREDIENTS

230G OF CREAM CHEESE

36 OREO COOKIES

WHITE/DARK/MILK
CHOCOLATE
(PICK YOUR FAVOURITE, OR
IN MY CASE, ALL OF THEM)

INSTRUCTIONS

1. CHINS UP; SMILES ON!

2. CRUSH THE OREOS FINELY (IT'S TIME TO
   RELEASE THAT ANGER!).

3. COMBINE FINELY CRUSHED OREOS WITH
   CREAM CHEESE (YES, USE YOUR HANDS).

4. IF THE MIXTURE IS TOO STICKY REFRIGERATE
   FOR 10 MINUTES.

5. IF NOT, JUMP INTO MAKING TINY BALLS
   OUT OF IT.

6. MELT THE CHOCOLATE.

7. ROLL THE BALLS INTO THE CHOCOLATE
   UNTIL IT LOOKS HEAVENLY.

8. REFRIGERATE UNTIL THE CHOCOLATE
   HARDENS.

9. GET READY, SET, ATTACK!

OREO SNOWMAN POPS

INGREDIENTS

OREO COOKIES
(DOUBLES WORK THE BEST)

WOODEN CAKE POP
STICKS

WHITE CHOCOLATE OR
REALLY THICK ICING

ORANGE TIC-TACS

BLACK FROSTING

INSTRUCTIONS

1. INSERT THE CAKE POP STICK INTO THE CREAM FILLING OF THE OREO COOKIES.

2. MELT THE WHITE CHOCOLATE AND POUR IT ON TOP OF THE OREO COOKIES, SETTING ASIDE TO COOL DOWN.

3. BEFORE IT COOLS DOWN, IMMEDIATELY PLACE THE ORANGE TIC-TACS IN THE CENTRE TO LOOK LIKE NOSES.

4. WHEN IT COOLS DOWN COMPLETELY, ADD THE EYES AND MOUTH DETAILS USING BLACK ICING.

5. YOU'VE JUST MADE THE CUTEST LOOKING SNOWMEN OUT OF OREO COOKIES!

BANANA COOKIES

MAKES 6 COOKIES

INGREDIENTS

2 BANANAS

2 CUPS OF OATS

INSTRUCTIONS

1. PREHEAT OVEN TO 180°C.

2. BLEND OATS IN A FOOD PROCESSOR UNTIL IT LOOKS LIKE THE CONSISTENCY OF FLOUR (IT DOESN'T HAVE TO BE PERFECT).

3. COMBINE MIXTURE WITH THE 2 MASHED BANANAS.

4. DROP LARGE SPOONS OF THE DOUGH ONTO A PIECE OF PARCHMENT PAPER AND BAKE FOR 10 TO 13 MINUTES.

RAPHA'S TIP

WHILE I LOVE HOW SIMPLE AND EASY THIS RECIPE IS, IF YOU HAVE THE CHANCE, TRY ADDING CHOCOLATE CHIP COOKIES, PEANUT BUTTER OR TOASTED ALMONDS. IT MAKES IT EVEN MORE DELICIOUS!

OREO COOKIE CUPCAKES

MAKES 6 CUPCAKES

INGREDIENTS

150G OF SELF-RAISING FLOUR

75G OF BUTTER

75G OF SUGAR

1 EGG

2 SPOONS OF COCOA POWDER

8 OREO COOKIES

INSTRUCTIONS

1. CREAM THE SUGAR, BUTTER AND EGG UNTIL LIGHT AND FLUFFY.

2. SIFT THE FLOUR IN AND STIR UNTIL COMBINED.

3. DIVIDE THE MIXTURE INTO TWO EQUAL PORTIONS.

4. ADD THE COCOA POWDER TO ONE OF THE MIXTURES.

5. SPOON THE WHITE MIXTURE INTO SOME CUPCAKE LINERS, TOPPING IT WITH AN OREO COOKIE.

6. NOW SPOON THE COCOA POWDER MIXTURE ON TOP.

7. BAKE FOR 15 TO 30 MINUTES AT 180°C.

8. TOP CUPCAKES WITH SOME CREAM CHEESE FROSTING (SEE PAGE 161) AND SPRINKLE THE REMAINING OREOS ON TOP. YOU CAN ALSO DECORATE IT WITH MINI-OREOS.

GINGERBREAD COOKIES

MAKES 30 COOKIES

INGREDIENTS

115G BUTTER

120G OF BROWN SUGAR

1 EGG

190G OF PLAIN FLOUR

½ TEASPOON OF BAKING SODA

1 TEASPOON OF GROUND GINGER

1 TEASPOON OF CINNAMON

INSTRUCTIONS

1. PREHEAT OVEN TO 175°C.

2. CREAM THE BUTTER AND BROWN SUGAR UNTIL SMOOTH.

3. ADD THE EGG AND STIR.

4. ADD THE REMAINING DRY INGREDIENTS AND COMBINE WITHOUT OVERMIXING.

5. COVER THE BOWL AND CHILL THE DOUGH FOR 15 TO 30 MINUTES.

6. ROLL OUT THE DOUGH ONTO A FLOURED SURFACE AND CUT THE COOKIES.

7. BAKE FOR 10 TO 12 MINUTES OR UNTIL GOLDEN.

M&M OREO COOKIE BARS

MAKES 12 COOKIES

INGREDIENTS

1 BATCH OF COOKIE
  DOUGH

12 OREO COOKIES

½ CUP OF M&MS

INSTRUCTIONS

1. PREHEAT OVEN TO 180°C.

2. STIR IN THE CRUSHED OREO COOKIES INTO THE COOKIE DOUGH.

3. SPREAD THE BATTER INTO A PREPARED PAN (PARCHMENT PAPER IS IDEAL), SMOOTHING THE TOP WITH A SPATULA.

4. SPRINKLE THE TOP WITH M&MS, PRESSING DOWN WITH FINGERS.

5. BAKE FOR 20 TO 25 MINUTES.

6. CUT AND SERVE THE MOST MAGICAL COOKIE BARS.

SCAN HERE

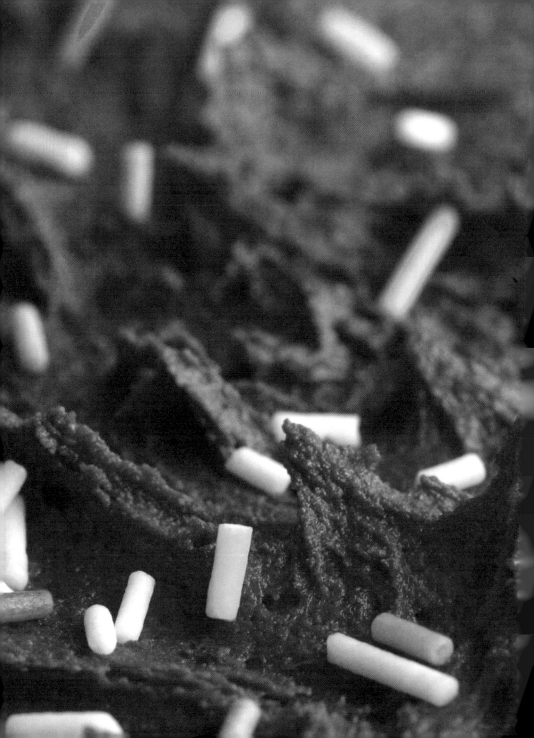

NO-BAKE NUTELLA AND -OREO CHEESECAKE-

MAKES ABOUT 4 INDIVIDUAL CHEESECAKES

INGREDIENTS

CRUST:

8 OREO COOKIES

1 TABLESPOON OF MELTED BUTTER

FILLING:

3 TEASPOONS OF WHITE SUGAR

$\frac{1}{3}$ OF A CUP AND 2 TEASPOONS OF HEAVY WHIPPING CREAM

$\frac{1}{3}$ OF A CUP AND 2 TEASPOONS OF NUTELLA

140G OR $\frac{5}{8}$ OF A CUP OF CREAM CHEESE

TOPPING:

WHIPPED CREAM

ADDITIONAL CRUSHED OREO COOKIES

TOASTED HAZELNUTS

INSTRUCTIONS

1. PUT THE OREO COOKIES IN A ZIP-LOCK BAG AND CRUSH THEM USING A ROLLING PIN.

2. ADD THE MELTED BUTTER AND SHAKE TO INCORPORATE.

3. IN A MEDIUM BOWL, WHIP THE CREAM WITH THE WHITE SUGAR UNTIL CONSISTENT.

4. IN ANOTHER BOWL, WHIP THE CREAM CHEESE UNTIL FLUFFY.

5. ADD THE NUTELLA AND WHIP UNTIL COMBINED.

6. IN INDIVIDUAL SERVING CUPS, CREATE A LAYER WITH THE CRUST AND SPOON THE NUTELLA FILLING ON TOP. FINISH BY DECORATING WITH SOME WHIPPED CREAM, CRUSHED OREO COOKIES AND TOASTED HAZELNUTS.

3 INGREDIENT BROWNIES

MAKES 8 MINI-BROWNIES

INGREDIENTS

½ CUP OF PLAIN FLOUR

1 CUP OF NUTELLA

2 EGGS

INSTRUCTIONS

1. IT'S REALLY IMPORTANT TO GREASE YOUR BAKING DISH AND LINE IT WITH PARCHMENT PAPER.

2. PREHEAT OVEN TO 180°C.

3. MIX ALL THE INGREDIENTS IN A LARGE BOWL BEFORE TRANSFERRING TO THE BAKING DISH.

4. BAKE FOR 15 MINUTES, OR UNTIL A TOOTH-PICK INSERTED INTO THE BROWNIE COMES OUT CLEAN.

5. LET THE BROWNIE COOL DOWN BEFORE CUTTING INTO IT.

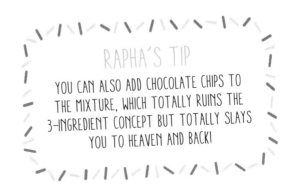

RAPHA'S TIP

YOU CAN ALSO ADD CHOCOLATE CHIPS TO THE MIXTURE, WHICH TOTALLY RUINS THE 3-INGREDIENT CONCEPT BUT TOTALLY SLAYS YOU TO HEAVEN AND BACK!

OREO POPCORN

SERVES 4

INGREDIENTS

12 OREO COOKIES

2 CUPS OF WHITE CHOCOLATE

5 CUPS OF POPCORN

INSTRUCTIONS

1. POP THE CORN IN A PAN, USING A LITTLE BIT OF VEGETABLE OIL. DO NOT HEAT IT FOR LONGER THAN 1 MINUTE OR IT WILL BURN.

2. PLACE THE POPCORN IN A LARGE BOWL.

3. PLACE THE OREO COOKIES IN A ZIP-LOCK BAG AND CRUSH THEM.

4. MELT THE WHITE CHOCOLATE IN THE MICROWAVE FOR 30 SECONDS, STIR AND REPEAT UNTIL SMOOTH.

5. POUR THE CHOCOLATE IN TO THE LARGE BOWL, COATING THE POPCORN.

6. ADD THE OREO COOKIES AND MIX.

RAPHA'S TIP

THIS IS THE PERFECT SNACK FOR A REALLY SCARY HORROR MOVIE WHEN ANY SOURCE OF COMFORT IS WELCOME!

SCAN HERE

CARAMEL POPCORN

INGREDIENTS

5 CUPS OF POPCORN

150G OF BROWN SUGAR

135G OF BUTTER

2 TABLESPOONS OF HONEY

INSTRUCTIONS

1. IN A PAN, POP THE CORN WITH A LITTLE BIT OF VEGETABLE OIL.

2. REMOVE THE POPCORN AND SET ASIDE.

3. IN THE SAME PAN, MELT THE BUTTER AND ADD THE BROWN SUGAR AND HONEY.

4. BRING TO A BOIL FOR 4 MINUTES.

5. TURN OFF THE HEAT AND ADD THE POP-CORN TO THE PAN, STIRRING TO COAT THE POPCORN EVENLY.

6. LET IT SIT FOR A FEW MINUTES TO COOL DOWN AND GET REALLY CRUNCHY.

7. BREAK THE POPCORN DOWN WITH YOUR HANDS AND IT'S READY TO SERVE.

EASIEST CARROT CUPCAKES

MAKES 12 CUPCAKES

INGREDIENTS

1 CUP OF FLOUR

2 CUPS OF GRATED CARROTS

⅔ OF A CUP OF OIL

⅔ OF A CUP OF SUGAR

2 EGGS

1 TEASPOON OF CINNAMON

1 TEASPOON OF BAKING SODA

1 TEASPOON OF BAKING POWDER

1 TEASPOON OF VANILLA EXTRACT

INSTRUCTIONS

1. PREHEAT OVEN TO 180°C AND PLACE THE CUPCAKE LINERS IN A MUFFIN TIN.

2. BEAT THE EGGS FOR A MINUTE AND ADD THE GRATED CARROTS, OIL AND VANILLA EXTRACT. STIR.

3. ADD THE REST OF THE INGREDIENTS AND STIR WELL WITHOUT OVER-MIXING.

4. FILL THE CUPS AND BAKE FOR ABOUT 15 MINUTES OR UNTIL EDGES TURN GOLDEN.

5. TOP THE CUPCAKES WITH CREAM CHEESE FROSTING.

6. READY TO SERVE AND ENJOY!

EDIBLE COOKIE DOUGH!

SERVES 4

INGREDIENTS

½ CUP OF BUTTER

2 TABLESPOONS OF MILK

1 CUP OF CHOCOLATE CHIPS

¾ CUP OF BROWN SUGAR

1 TEASPOON OF VANILLA EXTRACT

1 CUP OF PLAIN FLOUR

½ TEASPOON OF SALT

INSTRUCTIONS

1. CREAM TOGETHER THE BUTTER, SUGAR, VANILLA EXTRACT AND SALT.

2. ADD THE FLOUR AND MIX UNTIL YOU GET A CRUMB-LIKE CONSISTENCY.

3. ADD 2 TABLESPOONS OF MILK UNTIL THE MIXTURE LOOKS LIKE COOKIE DOUGH.

4. ADD THE CHOCOLATE CHIPS AND IT'S READY TO EAT.

RAPHA'S TIP

IF YOU LIKE COOKIE DOUGH AS MUCH AS I DO YOU WILL LOVE TO EAT THIS STRAIGHT FROM THE BOWL OR (IF YOU'RE A LITTLE BIT MORE SENSIBLE!) YOU CAN SCOOP IT ON TO SOME ICE CREAM.

3 INGREDIENT NUTELLA MUFFINS

MAKES 12 SMALL MUFFINS OR 6 REGULAR ONES

INGREDIENTS

1 JAR OF NUTELLA

2 EGGS

11 TABLESPOONS OF
SELF-RAISING FLOUR

INSTRUCTIONS

1. SET CUPCAKE LINERS ON YOUR MUFFIN TRAY.

2. MIX ALL THE INGREDIENTS IN A BOWL.

3. BAKE FOR 20 TO 30 MINUTES AT 170°C, OR UNTIL A TOOTHPICK INSERTED INTO THE MUFFINS COMES OUT CLEAN.

RAPHA'S TIP

THIS RECIPE IS PERFECT FOR THOSE TIMES WHEN YOU'RE CRAVING SOMETHING SWEET BUT YOU DON'T WANT TO SPEND TWO HOURS WASHING UP DISHES!

COOK YOUR FRIED EGGS INSIDE AN ONION RING FOR A PERFECTLY ROUND SHAPE.

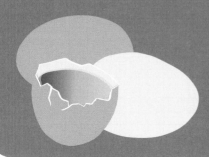

ROLL SOME PUFF PASTRY AROUND A CADBURY CREME EGG FOR A QUICK AND DELICIOUS CROISSANT.

CHOCOLATE AND CORNFLAKE CAKES

INGREDIENTS

50G OF BUTTER

50G OF DARK CHOCOLATE

50G OF MILK CHOCOLATE

2 TABLESPOONS OF GOLDEN SYRUP (OR MAPLE SYRUP)

100G OF CORNFLAKES

INSTRUCTIONS

1. MELT THE BUTTER, CHOCOLATE AND GOLDEN SYRUP IN A PAN WITHOUT LETTING IT COME TO A BOIL.

2. TURN DOWN THE TEMPERATURE AND ADD THE CORNFLAKES.

3. STIR WITHOUT BREAKING THE CORNFLAKES TOO MUCH.

4. POUR THE MIXTURE INTO 10 CUPCAKE CASES.

5. YOU CAN DECORATE THE CAKES WITH M&M'S, SMARTIES OR ANY OTHER COLOURFUL CANDY.

RAPHA'S TIP

YOU CAN TRY REPLACING THE CORNFLAKES WITH OTHER CEREAL! IT MIGHT TASTE DELICIOUS OR IT MIGHT GO WRONG BUT ALWAYS WORTH THE ADVENTURE :)

SCAN HERE

NOT SURE WHERE IT FITS

ZEBRA CAKE

SERVES 6

INGREDIENTS

4 EGGS

250G OF GRANULATED SUGAR

250ML MILK

250ML OF VEGETABLE OIL

300G ALL-PURPOSE FLOUR

2 TEASPOONS VANILLA EXTRACT

3 TEASPOONS BAKING POWDER

2 TABLESPOONS DARK COCOA POWDER

BLACK FOOD COLOURING (OPTIONAL)

INSTRUCTIONS

1. COMBINE EGGS AND SUGAR. BEAT UNTIL THE MIXTURE IS CREAMY AND LIGHT.

2. ADD MILK AND OIL.

3. GRADUALLY ADD THE FLOUR AND BAKING POWDER TO THE WET INGREDIENTS AND BEAT JUST UNTIL THE BATTER IS SMOOTH (DO NOT OVERBEAT!).

4. DIVIDE THE MIXTURE INTO 2 EQUAL PORTIONS. ADD VANILLA FLAVOURING TO ONE. ADD COCOA POWDER INTO ANOTHER AND MIX WELL.

5. PREHEAT THE OVEN TO 180°C

6. GREASE PAN.

7. SCOOP 3 TABLESPOONS OF PLAIN BATTER INTO THE MIDDLE OF THE BAKING PAN. THEN SCOOP 3 TABLESPOONS OF COCOA BATTER AND POUR IT INTO THE CENTRE, ON TOP OF THE PLAIN BATTER. REPEAT.

8. BAKE IN THE OVEN FOR ABOUT 40 MINUTES. DO NOT OPEN THE OVEN DOOR FOR AT LEAST THE FIRST 20 MINUTES.

9. ENJOY THE COOLEST CAKE IN EXISTENCE!

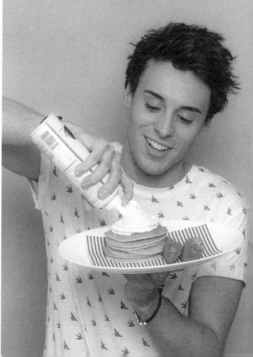

THE BEST AMERICAN PANCAKES

MAKES 8

INGREDIENTS

180ML OF MILK

20ML OF WHITE VINEGAR

125G OF FLOUR

25G OF WHITE SUGAR

5G OF BAKING POWDER

2G OF BAKING SODA

5G OF SALT

1 EGG

INSTRUCTIONS

1. COMBINE MILK WITH VINEGAR IN A SMALL BOWL AND SET ASIDE FOR A FEW MINUTES.

2. COMBINE FLOUR, SUGAR, BAKING POWDER, BAKING SODA AND SALT.

3. WHISK THE EGG INTO THE MILK-AND-VINEGAR MIXTURE.

4. COMBINE THE TWO MIXTURES AND WHISK UNTIL SMOOTH.

5. GREASE A FRYING PAN WITH SOME BUTTER AND COOK THE PANCAKES ON MEDIUM HEAT UNTIL FLUFFY AND GOLDEN.

6. WHEN YOU SEE TINY BUBBLES ON THE SURFACE, TIME TO GIVE IT AN EPIC FLIP.

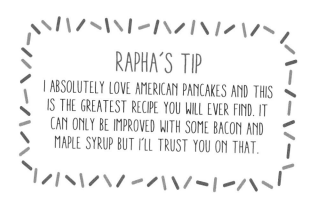

RAPHA'S TIP

I ABSOLUTELY LOVE AMERICAN PANCAKES AND THIS IS THE GREATEST RECIPE YOU WILL EVER FIND. IT CAN ONLY BE IMPROVED WITH SOME BACON AND MAPLE SYRUP BUT I'LL TRUST YOU ON THAT.

USING A SMALL CUP,
MAKE A CIRCLE
IN YOUR
RAW BURGER
FOR A PERFECTLY-SIZED
LOCATION FOR
YOUR FRIED EGG.

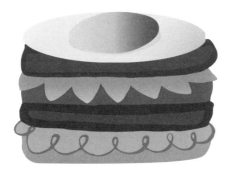

USE STRAWS TO REMOVE STRAWBERRY STEMS WITH 100% ACCURACY

NUTELLA PANCAKE CAKE

SERVES 4

INGREDIENTS

240G OF SIFTED PLAIN FLOUR

4 EGGS

400ML OF MILK WITH 150ML OF WATER

25G OF MELTED BUTTER

SALT

WHIPPED CREAM

NUTELLA

INSTRUCTIONS

1. SIFT THE FLOUR AND SALT INTO A LARGE BOWL AND WHISK THE EGGS ONE AT A TIME.

2. WHEN IT GETS REALLY LUMPY, ADD THE MILK AND WATER MIXTURE GRADUALLY UNTIL IT BECOMES SMOOTH. FINISH THE MIXTURE BY ADDING THE MELTED BUTTER AND STIRRING.

3. COOK IN A MEDIUM-TO-HIGH HEAT PAN, USING NON-STICK SPRAY OR BUTTER.

4. THIS SHOULD ALLOW YOU TO MAKE 12 (OR MORE) LARGE PANCAKES.

5. NOW IT'S TIME TO STACK THEM UP BY ALTERNATIVELY PLACING WHIPPED CREAM AND NUTELLA BETWEEN THE LAYERS.

6. TOP THE CAKE WITH SOME MORE WHIPPED CREAM AND COCOA POWDER.

7. WHEN YOU CUT INTO IT, YOU SHOULD BE ABLE TO SEE ALL THE AMAZING LAYERS OF DELICIOUSNESS. NOT YOUR CONVENTIONAL PANCAKE, RIGHT?

RAPHA'S TIP

THIS IS A GREAT OPTION FOR A BIRTHDAY CAKE IF YOU'RE NOT REALLY INTO SPONGE CAKES!

CRISPY BACON AND CHEESE ROLL-UPS

SERVES 4

INGREDIENTS

10 SLICES OF BREAD

10 SLICES OF YOUR
FAVOURITE CHEESE

10 SLICES OF PRE-
COOKED BACON

INSTRUCTIONS

1. WITH THE HELP OF A ROLLING PIN, FLATTEN THE SLICES OF BREAD.

2. PLACE THE CHEESE ON THE BREAD AND ROLL UP SO THAT THE CHEESE STAYS IN THE CENTRE.

3. WRAP EACH ROLL IN BACON AND SECURE IT WITH SOME TOOTHPICKS.

4. COOK IN A FRYING PAN ON A MEDIUM HEAT UNTIL THE BACON CRISPS UP AND THE CHEESE HAS MELTED.

5. ENJOY WHILE IT'S HOT!

MAC 'N' CHEESE IN A MUG

INGREDIENTS

1 CUP OF MACARONI PASTA

1 CUP OF MILK

1 CUP OF GRATED CHEDDAR CHEESE

¼ TEASPOON OF GARLIC POWDER

¼ TEASPOON OF ONION POWDER

INSTRUCTIONS

1. MICROWAVE THE MACARONI PASTA IN A MUG WITH THE MILK FOR 3 MINUTES, STIRRING EVERY 1 MINUTE. MAKE SURE THE NOODLES DON'T STICK TO THE BOTTOM.

2. GET RID OF ANY UNWANTED LIQUID. ADD THE CHEESE AND POWDERS TO YOUR MUG AND MICROWAVE IT FOR AN EXTRA 30 SECONDS TO MELT.

3. ENJOY!

FRENCH TOAST ROLL-UPS

MAKES 8 ROLL-UPS

INGREDIENTS

8 SLICES OF WHITE
SANDWICH BREAD

CREAM CHEESE

STRAWBERRIES

NUTELLA

2 TABLESPOONS OF MILK

65G OF WHITE SUGAR

1 TEASPOON OF
GROUND CINNAMON

INSTRUCTIONS

1. WHISK THE EGGS AND MILK UNTIL COMBINED IN ONE BOWL.

2. MIX THE SUGAR AND CINNAMON IN A DIFFERENT BOWL.

3. FLATTEN THE BREAD WITH THE HELP OF A ROLLING PIN.

4. SPREAD YOUR FAVOURITE FILLING ON TO THE BREAD (CREAM CHEESE, NUTELLA, STRAWBERRIES) AND ROLL THE BREAD TIGHTLY.

5. DIP EACH ROLL INTO THE EGG MIXTURE AND COOK UNTIL CRISPY AND BROWN.

6. FINISH BY DIPPING THEM STRAIGHT INTO THE SUGAR AND CINNAMON MIXTURE.

NO-BAKE NUTELLA CHEESECAKE

SERVES 6

INGREDIENTS

250G OF PLAIN BISCUITS

100G OF CRUSHED HAZELNUTS

80G OF SOFT BUTTER

400G OF NUTELLA

500G OF CREAM CHEESE

80G OF ICING SUGAR

INSTRUCTIONS

1. LINE A PAN WITH SOME PARCHMENT PAPER.

2. CRUMBLE THE BISCUITS IN A ZIPLOCK BAG AND COMBINE WITH THE BUTTER, HAZELNUTS AND 1 TABLESPOON OF NUTELLA.

3. PRESS ONTO THE PAN AND LET IT CHILL.

4. BEAT THE CREAM CHEESE, THE REMAINING NUTELLA AND THE ICING SUGAR UNTIL WELL COMBINED.

5. POUR IT ON TOP OF THE BISCUIT BASE AND CHILL FOR A FEW HOURS OR UNTIL SOLID.

RAPHA'S TIP

NO BAKE RECIPES ARE THE BEST BECAUSE YOU DON'T HAVE TO STRESS OVER COOKING TIMES! PLAY YOUR FAVOURITE MUSIC AND ENJOY SOME QUALITY KITCHEN TIME :)

SMORES HOT CHOCOLATE

INGREDIENTS

100G OF DARK
CHOCOLATE

1 TABLESPOON OF
BROWN SUGAR

500ML OF MILK AND
CINNAMON

MARSHMALLOWS

BUTTER BISCUITS
(OR IDEALLY GRAHAM
CRACKERS!)

INSTRUCTIONS

1. TO MAKE THE HOT CHOCOLATE, MELT THE DARK CHOCOLATE, A GENEROUS SPOONFUL OF BROWN SUGAR, 500ML OF MILK AND CINNAMON. BRING IT TO A BOIL TO THICKEN UP A LITTLE BIT.

2. ROLL A MARSHMALLOW ON THE EDGE OF YOUR MUG SO IT GETS MESSY AND STICKY. ADD CRUSHED BUTTER BISCUITS SO THEY WILL STICK TO IT.

3. POUR HOT CHOCOLATE INTO THE MUG AND TOP IT WITH MINI MARSHMALLOWS.

4. PLACE IT IN THE OVEN FOR A SHORT TIME IF YOU WANT THE MARSHMALLOWS TO GO BROWN AND GOLDEN.

5. ENJOY THE DELICIOUSNESS.

RAPHA'S TIP

WHEN I MAKE THIS RECIPE I ALWAYS TOP IT UP WITH SOME CHOCOLATE PANCAKE SYRUP FOR A FINAL TOUCH OF HEAVEN.

NUTELLA MILKSHAKE

INGREDIENTS

3 CUPS OF VANILLA ICE CREAM

¼ CUP OF NUTELLA

½ CUP OF MILK

1 KINDER BUENO

WHIPPED CREAM

NUTELLA FOR DRIZZLING

INSTRUCTIONS

1. MEASURE ALL THE INGREDIENTS AND PLACE IN THE BLENDER. STOP IT WHEN IT'S CREAMY AND YOU NO LONGER SEE CHUNKS OF THE KINDER BUENO.

2. POUR INTO 2 KILNER JARS AND TOP IT WITH WHIPPED CREAM AND NUTELLA.

3. ALTERNATIVELY YOU CAN USE SPRINKLES ON THE EDGES OF YOUR SERVING GLASS FOR A TOUCH OF COLOUR.

RAPHA'S TIP

YOU COULD ALSO CHANGE NUTELLA FOR OREOS. SCAN THE PAGE TO SEE THIS IN ACTION!

SCAN HERE

MY MUM'S CHOCOLATE CAKE

SERVES 8

INGREDIENTS

6 EGGS

250G OF BUTTER

300G OF SUGAR

250G OF SELF-
RAISING FLOUR

250G PLAIN
CHOCOLATE BAR

MILK

INSTRUCTIONS

1. MELT HALF OF THE CHOCOLATE BAR, ADDING ENOUGH MILK TO MAKE THE MIXTURE SMOOTH, BUT NOT ENOUGH TO MAKE IT RUNNY.

2. ALLOW IT TO COOL A LITTLE BIT. WHIP 6 EGG WHITES UNTIL WHITE, FLUFFY AND CONSISTENT. SET ASIDE.

3. IN A DIFFERENT BOWL, CREAM THE SUGAR, BUTTER AND EGG YOLKS.

4. ADD THE MELTED CHOCOLATE AND MIX WELL.

5. ADD THE FLOUR GRADUALLY. DON'T OVER MIX IT.

6. ADD THE EGG WHITES TO THE MIXTURE AND INCORPORATE IT.

7. COOK FOR 45 MINUTES TO AN HOUR.

8. MELT THE REST OF THE CHOCOLATE WITH A LITTLE BIT OF MILK TO POUR OVER THE CAKE.

MARSHMALLOW RICE KRISPIE TREATS

MAKES 20 TREATS

INGREDIENTS

60G OF BUTTER

210G OF MINIATURE MARSHMALLOWS

140G OF CRISP RICE CEREAL

INSTRUCTIONS

1. MELT BUTTER ON A LOW HEAT AND ADD MARSHMALLOWS UNTIL MELTED AND WELL BLENDED.

2. ADD CEREAL AND STIR.

3. POUR MIXTURE ONTO A GREASED SQUARE PAN AND USE PARCHMENT PAPER TO PRESS IT DOWN.

4. ALLOW IT TO COOL AND CUT INTO SLICES.

RAPHA'S TIP

FOOD COLOURING IS THE HERO IN THIS RECIPE, ADD IT TO THE MARSHMALLOW MIXTURE AND BE CREATIVE!

SCAN HERE

STRAWBERRY AND LEMON SLURPEES

MAKES 3 – 4 SLURPEES

INGREDIENTS

1 PACKET OF LEMONADE KOOL-AID

¾ CUP OF WHITE SUGAR

6 STRAWBERRIES

2 CUPS OF FIZZY WATER

2 AND ½ CUPS OF ICE CUBES

JUICE OF HALF A LEMON

INSTRUCTIONS

1. PLACE ALL INGREDIENTS IN A BLENDER AND BLEND UNTIL ICE IS CRUSHED AND INGREDIENTS COMBINED.

2. SERVE IN MASON JARS AND DON'T FORGET THE ESSENTIAL COOL STRAWS.

RAPHA'S TIP

THIS IS THE PERFECT DRINK FOR A WARM SUMMER DAY WHEN YOU'RE BORED AND IT'S WAY TOO HOT TO GO OUTSIDE!

BANANA & PEANUT -BUTTER SUNDAES-

MAKES 2 SERVINGS

INGREDIENTS

3 BANANAS

2 TABLESPOONS OF SMOOTH PEANUT BUTTER

¼ TEASPOON OF VANILLA EXTRACT

TOPPINGS:

MELTED CHOCOLATE

TOASTED NUTS

SPRINKLES

INSTRUCTIONS

1. SLICE THE BANANAS AND FREEZE THEM OVERNIGHT IN A ZIP-LOCK BAG.

2. REMOVE THE BANANA FROM THE FREEZER AND LET IT REST AT ROOM TEMPERATURE FOR A FEW MINUTES.

3. ADD THE BANANAS, PEANUT BUTTER AND VANILLA EXTRACT TO YOUR BLENDER AND COMBINE ON LOW SPEED.

4. SCOOP INTO BOWLS AND SERVE IT WITH ICE CREAM AND YOUR FAVOURITE MELTED CHOCOLATE AND TOPPINGS.

SALTED CARAMEL MILKSHAKE

MAKES ABOUT 3 MILKSHAKES

INGREDIENTS

2 CUPS OF VANILLA ICE CREAM

½ CUP OF MILK

2 TABLESPOONS OF CARAMEL SYRUP

1 TEASPOON OF SALT

1 BAR OF TWIX CHOCOLATE

WHIPPED CREAM

CHOCOLATE SHAVINGS FOR DECORATION

INSTRUCTIONS

1. ADD ALL THE INGREDIENTS TO YOUR BLENDER APART FROM THE WHIPPED CREAM AND THE CHOCOLATE SHAVINGS.

2. WHEN IT LOOKS RICH AND SMOOTH POUR IT INTO YOUR GLASS OR MASON JAR.

3. DECORATE USING WHIPPED CREAM AND CHOCOLATE SHAVINGS.

4. ENJOY ONE OF THE MOST DELICIOUS MILKSHAKES EVER CREATED!

2 INGREDIENT NUTELLA POPSICLES

MAKES ABOUT 3 POPSICLES

INGREDIENTS

1 CUP OF WHOLE MILK

½ CUP OF NUTELLA

INSTRUCTIONS

1. PLACE MILK AND NUTELLA IN A BLENDER AND MAKE SURE IT'S WELL COMBINED.

2. POUR MIXTURE INTO POPSICLE MOULDS AND FREEZE FOR 2 HOURS.

RAPHA'S TIP

YOU CAN ADD TOASTED HAZELNUTS OR RAINBOW SPRINKLES TO MAKE THEM LOOK EXTRA DELICIOUS ONCE YOU TAKE THE POPSICLES FROM THE FREEZER.

RICE KRISPIE CHOCOLATE BALLS

MAKES 10 BARS

INGREDIENTS

2 CUPS OF CREAMY PEANUT BUTTER

3 CUPS OF RICE KRISPIES

3 CUPS OF ICING SUGAR

¼ CUP OF MELTED BUTTER

3 PACKETS OF MILK CHOCOLATE CHIPS

INSTRUCTIONS

1. MIX TOGETHER THE PEANUT BUTTER, RICE KRISPIES, ICING SUGAR AND MELTED BUTTER.

2. MAKE TINY BALLS WITH THE MIXTURE.

3. DIP THEM INTO THE MELTED MILK CHOCOLATE CHIPS.

4. PLACE THEM ONTO A COOKIE SHEET AND LET THEM REST IN THE FREEZER UNTIL THE CHOCOLATE HARDENS COMPLETELY.

BASICS

SCAN HERE

VANILLA SPONGE CAKE

SERVES 8

INGREDIENTS

4 EGGS

250G WHITE SUGAR

250G CUP OF MILK

250G OF VEGETABLE OIL

300G OF ALL-PURPOSE FLOUR

2 TEASPOONS OF VANILLA EXTRACT

3 TEASPOONS OF BAKING POWDER

INSTRUCTIONS

1. COMBINE EGGS AND SUGAR UNTIL YOU HAVE A CREAMY AND LIGHT MIXTURE.

2. ADD MILK AND OIL, AND INCORPORATE.

3. GRADUALLY ADD FLOUR AND BAKING POWDER AND BEAT IN UNTIL SMOOTH WITHOUT OVER-MIXING.

4. POUR INTO A GREASED TIN AND BAKE AT 180°C FOR 30 TO 40 MINUTES.

CHOCOLATE CAKE

SERVES 8

INGREDIENTS

375G OF WHITE SUGAR

220G OF PLAIN FLOUR

65G OF UNSWEETENED COCOA POWDER

2 EGGS

235ML OF MILK

120ML OF VEGETABLE OIL

2 TEASPOONS OF VANILLA EXTRACT

220ML OF BOILING WATER

1 AND ½ TEASPOONS OF BAKING SODA

1 AND ½ TEASPOONS OF BAKING POWDER

1 TEASPOON OF SALT

INSTRUCTIONS

1. PREHEAT OVEN TO 180°C.

2. GREASE TWO CAKE PANS.

3. STIR TOGETHER THE SUGAR, FLOUR, UN-SWEETENED COCOA, BAKING POWDER, BAKING SODA AND SALT.

4. ADD EGGS, MILK, OIL AND VANILLA EXTRACT, AND MIX IT ALL TOGETHER.

5. STIR THE BOILING WATER IN AND DON'T WORRY IF IT LOOKS TOO RUNNY.

6. BAKE THE CAKE MIXTURE FOR 30 TO 35 MINUTES AND LET IT COOL DOWN BEFORE YOU REMOVE IT FROM THE CAKE PAN.

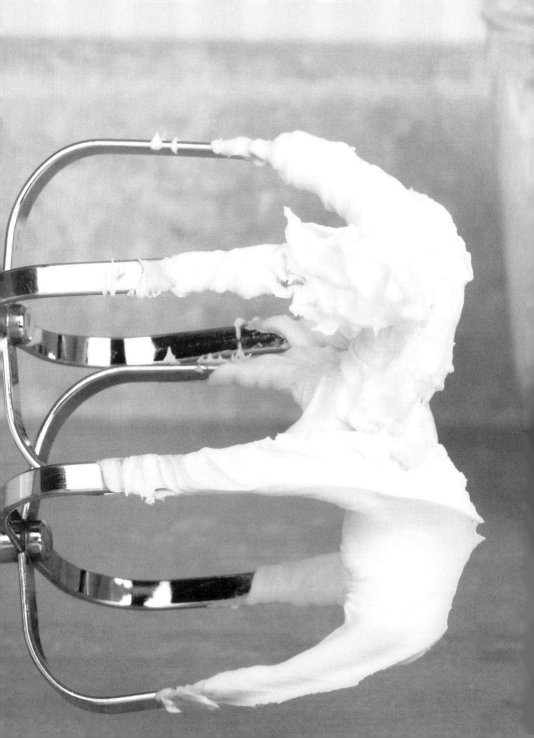

VANILLA FROSTING

150G OF SOFTENED BUTTER

500G OF ICING SUGAR

30ML OF MILK

2 TEASPOONS OF VANILLA
EXTRACT

INSTRUCTIONS

1. IN A BOWL, CREAM THE BUTTER, MILK AND ICING SUGAR FOR 4 TO 5 MINUTES USING AN ELECTRIC MIXER.

2. ONCE IT'S LIGHT AND FLUFFY, ADD THE VANILLA FROSTING AND MAKE SURE IT'S WELL INCORPORATED.

3. YOUR MIXTURE IS READY! SPREAD IT ON COOKIES OR CAKES, OR EAT IT DIRECTLY FROM A BOWL WITH A SPOON!

CREAM CHEESE FROSTING

INGREDIENTS

- 2 PACKETS OF CREAM CHEESE
- 110G OF SOFTENED BUTTER
- 260G OF ICING SUGAR
- 2 TEASPOONS OF VANILLA EXTRACT

INSTRUCTIONS

1. IT'S REALLY IMPORTANT THAT YOU START OFF BY SIFTING THE ICING SUGAR.

2. WHIP THE CREAM CHEESE AND BUTTER UNTIL SMOOTH.

3. ADD THE VANILLA EXTRACT.

4. GRADUALLY INCORPORATE THE ICING SUGAR, ADD MORE IF NECESSARY.

5. STORE IT IN A COLD PLACE TO PREVENT IT FROM GOING TOO SOFT.

RAPHA'S TIP

THIS RECIPE IS IDEAL FOR ANYTHING WITH CHOCOLATE. IT IS THE BEST COMBINATION YOU WILL EVER TRY!

MARSHMALLOW FONDANT

INGREDIENTS

450G OF PLAIN MARSHMALLOWS

900G OF ICING SUGAR

1 AND ½ TABLE-SPOONS OF WATER

INSTRUCTIONS

1. MELT THE MARSHMALLOWS IN THE MICRO-WAVE FOR ABOUT 30 SECONDS.

2. ADD THE WATER AND STIR WELL USING A GREASED SPOON.

3. CARRY ON MELTING FOR 30-SECOND INTER-VALS UNTIL YOU REACH A SMOOTH MIXTURE.

4. GRADUALLY ADD THE ICING SUGAR AND MIX UNTIL THE 450G OF MARSHMALLOWS ARE INCORPORATED.

5. YOU CAN NOW WORK THE MIXTURE USING ICING SUGAR WHENEVER IT GETS TOO STICKY.

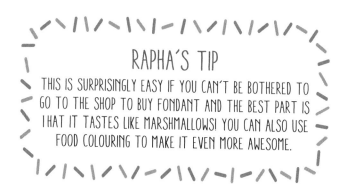

RAPHA'S TIP

THIS IS SURPRISINGLY EASY IF YOU CAN'T BE BOTHERED TO GO TO THE SHOP TO BUY FONDANT AND THE BEST PART IS THAT IT TASTES LIKE MARSHMALLOWS! YOU CAN ALSO USE FOOD COLOURING TO MAKE IT EVEN MORE AWESOME.

SIMPLE CRISPY SUGAR COOKIES

MAKES 35 COOKIES

INGREDIENTS

115G OF BUTTER

120ML OF VEGETABLE OIL

90G OF ICING SUGAR

100G OF WHITE SUGAR

1 EGG

2 TEASPOONS OF VANILLA EXTRACT

280G OF PLAIN FLOUR

½ TEASPOON OF BAKING SODA

INSTRUCTIONS

1. PREHEAT OVEN TO 180°C.

2. IN A LARGE BOWL, CREAM THE BUTTER, OIL, ICING SUGAR AND WHITE SUGAR UNTIL LIGHT AND FLUFFY.

3. BEAT THE EGGS IN ONE AT A TIME, ALONG WITH THE VANILLA EXTRACT.

4. COMBINE THE FLOUR AND BAKING SODA AND STIR IT INTO THE MIXTURE.

5. MAKE TINY BALLS OUT OF THE DOUGH AND FLATTEN THEM WITH A FORK.

6. BAKE FOR 10 TO 12 MINUTES AND SPRINKLE WITH WHITE SUGAR WHILE IT COOLS DOWN.

RAPHA'S TIP

THESE COOKIES ARE SO LIGHT AND CRISPY, AND I PROMISE THEY WILL MELT IN YOUR MOUTH!

CLASSIC PIZZA DOUGH

MAKES 1 LARGE PIZZA OR SERVES 4

INGREDIENTS

7G OF ACTIVE DRY YEAST

30ML OF OLIVE OIL

6G OF SALT

8G OF WHITE SUGAR

230ML OF WARM WATER

275G OF BREAD FLOUR

INSTRUCTIONS

1. DISSOLVE YEAST IN WARM WATER AND LET IT STAND FOR 15 MINUTES.

2. COMBINE BREAD FLOUR, OLIVE OIL, WHITE SUGAR, SALT AND DRY YEAST MIXTURE.

3. STIR TO COMBINE AND BEAT UNTIL THE DOUGH IS STIFF.

4. COVER AND LET IT DOUBLE IN VOLUME FOR 30 TO 45 MINUTES.

5. PREHEAT OVEN TO 175°C.

6. ROLL OUT DOUGH AND WORK IT INTO A PIZZA-CRUST SHAPE.

7. BAKE FOR 20 TO 30 MINUTES WITH YOUR FAVOURITE TOPPINGS.

STURDY
TONGS CAN HELP YOU
JUICE
A LEMON.

CUT THE BOTTOM OF A CUPCAKE AND THEN USE IT TO TURN IT INTO A SANDWICH.

CUT THE BOTTOM OF A CUPCAKE AND THEN USE IT TO TURN IT INTO A SANDWICH.

ACKNOWLEDGEMENTS

I WOULD LIKE TO THANK THE BLINK TEAM, INCLUDING EMILY ROUGH, JOEL SIMONS AND LIZZIE DORNEY-KINGDOM FOR WORKING SO HARD WITH ME ON THIS BOOK. AND ESPECIALLY CLARE TILLYER, WHO IMMEDIATELY UNDERSTOOD THE COLOURFUL VISION I HAD IN MY HEAD AND HELPED ME BRING IT TO LIFE.

I WOULD ALSO LIKE TO THANK EVERYBODY AT FLIPSIDE TALENT AND IN PARTICULAR MIKE COOK AND MARIANNE TURTON WHO BELIEVED IN THIS CONCEPT FROM THE VERY BEGINNING AND DIDN'T GIVE UP ON ME THROUGHOUT ALL THE DEADLINES (EVEN THE ONES I MISSED - OOPS). THANK YOU FOR ALSO SHOWING UP AT MY HOUSE AND TAKING MUG CAKES AND COOKIES AS SERIOUSLY AS I DO. I'LL FOREVER BE GRATEFUL FOR THE TWO OF YOU.

A HUGE `THANK YOU' TO ALL OF MY FRIENDS WHO HAVE STOOD BY ME FOR THE LAST YEAR, EVEN WHEN I COULDN'T GO OUTSIDE BECAUSE I WAS WORKING WEEKEND AFTER WEEKEND. FIZZY, VANIA, INES, CRAIG, HERMANN AND SO MANY MORE THAT WILL PROBABLY HAVE A GO AT ME BECAUSE I FORGOT THEIR NAMES. I AM SO SORRY IN ADVANCE! THANK YOU FOR MAKING ME SMILE EVEN ON THE MOST STRESSFUL DAYS.

THE BIGGEST THANKS TO MY FAMILY - MY MUM AND DAD WHO GAVE ME THE BEST CHILDHOOD AND SUPPORT ME MORE AND MORE EVERY DAY. AND MY SISTER JOANA, WHO IS SUCH A LITTLE POOP-FACE BUT HELPS ME FILM SO MANY OF MY VIDEOS. I LOVE YOU THREE.

THE LAST `THANK YOU' IS FOR YOU. WHETHER YOU ARE A READER OR AN AVID VIEWER OF MY YOUTUBE CHANNEL. WHETHER YOU FOUND OUT ABOUT ME TODAY OR TWO YEARS AGO. THANK YOU FOR SUPPORTING ME AND JOINING MY COLOURFUL LITTLE WORLD. I OWE MY HAPPIEST MEMORIES TO YOU AND I WILL NEVER FORGET THAT. REAL FRIENDS, ONLINE FRIENDS... IT DOESN'T MATTER. WE'RE SIMPLY FRIENDS AND THAT MEANS THE WORLD TO ME. THANK YOU.